TAKE TWO: SKILL-BUILDING SKITS You Have Time to Do!

Active, Engaging Tier 2 Interventions for Secondary Students

by

Cindi Dodd, M.Ed.

BOYS TOWN Press®

Boys Town, Nebraska

Take Two: Skill-Building Skits You Have Time to Do!
Copyright © 2014 by Father Flanagan's Boys' Home

ISBN 978-1-934490-56-3

Published by Boys Town Press
14100 Crawford St.
Boys Town, Nebraska 68010

Printed in the United States
10 9 8 7 6 5 4 3 2 1

For a Boys Town Press catalog, call 1-800-282-6657
or visit our website: BoysTownPress.org

Boys Town Press is the publishing division of Boys Town, a national organization serving children and families

Table of Contents

Why Should I Buy This Book?
AN INTRODUCTORY SKIT FOR TEACHERS

NARRATOR: *Sara Jones comes into the teachers' lounge, grabs a cup of coffee and sits down next to John Meyer, who's reading the paper.*

SARA: Honestly, John, I am at my wits' end.

JOHN: *(Slowly puts the paper down and answers with a slight smile.)* What's the emergency today, Sara?

SARA: I just about had my face knocked off when one of the eighth-graders slammed the door without looking. I know it was probably an accident but he just walked on and didn't even say he was sorry. What has happened to manners? What's happened to social skills? I just feel like kids are coming to school not knowing the common things they used to know.

JOHN: I know what you mean. This morning I bet I said "Hi" to twenty kids in the hall and the majority didn't even answer.

SARA: Oh, that happens all the time. I really want to address this, but with all the testing and expectations we have any more, there just isn't much time.

JOHN: And students don't even seem that interested in talking about social skills, let alone using them.

NARRATOR: *Jane Morris, the ninth-grade math teacher, has been sitting nearby reading a book. She looks up and joins in the conversation.*

JANE: Not to interrupt your conversation, but have you guys seen this book? *(Holds up,* Take Two: Skill-Building Skits You Have Time to Do!*)*

JOHN AND SARA: No, what is it?

JANE: Well, it's a new book written by a gal who has spent twenty-five years in the trenches. She was a classroom teacher and Dean of Students at a secondary school so she knows what we're going through. It's a book of short skits you can do with kids that revolve around the Boys Town Social Skills. She's even included discussion questions and activities so you can just use it, fast and easy.

SARA: Can I see that? Kids love drama... in more ways than one. But to have skits all prepared and zeroed in on the social skills we want to reinforce is great!

JOHN: I agree... This looks like just what we need.

JANE: Yes, and after all the money I've spent on books just to find out that the activities were too complicated or took too long, it's nice to find something practical and fun.

SARA: I'm ordering *Take Two: Skill-Building Skits You Have Time to Do!* from the Boys Town Press® right now. You guys should do the same.

....

NARRATOR: Take Two: Skill-Building Skits You Have Time to Do! *will help you teach and reinforce the social skills you want to see in your secondary students. The skits engage, the questions stimulate conversation and the activities allow real-life application. This is a book by a secondary educator for secondary educators. It's a book for those who want to teach their students valuable social skills but don't have much time.*

....

Benefits of Implementing this Program...

- It's great for teaching secondary social skills or character programming.

- It's flexible. Use one activity, more than one activity or skip through activities as your time allows.

- Skits are developmentally appropriate for secondary students and are ready to go.

- The questions elicit discussion, which secondary students love.

- It can be used in your classroom, conference advisement, Tier 2 interventions, homerooms or detention programs.

- It's easy to use.

More about the Skills and the Skits

The Boys Town Education Model® includes a series of specific life skills and expectations. Directly teaching these skills, especially in the secondary school setting, may need to be done in a limited amount of time as more and more emphasis is placed on core classes. Keeping in mind the developmental level of secondary students, who learn by doing, this book of skits actively involves young people in the skill, showing inappropriate behaviors along with modeling positive replacement behaviors. It also gives students an opportunity to verbalize, summarize and write down what they have seen, and apply it to their own classroom experiences.

The skits included in this book are purposefully short and straightforward. They give the middle-level learner opportunities to participate in the drama or serve as a member of the "jury" to determine the right or wrong aspects of the behaviors. Add a box of simple costume pieces and you have a vehicle for not only teaching 21 Boys Town social skills but also involving students in a process that enables them to internalize positive behavioral choices.

How to Use the Skill-Building Materials (book, worksheets, posters)

Start each skit activity by assigning roles in the skit to the students in your class. For example, one student will be the Teacher and two students will play the part of students. The rest of the class serves as the "audience" and "jury." You (the teacher) always play the role of the Narrator.

If time allows, have the "cast" for the skit read through their lines before presenting it to the class. This will help students become familiar with their parts and help make the skit more realistic.

Once a skit is completed, hand out copies of the appropriate worksheet (located on the enclosed CD) to students so they can write down what they observed (What's Right?; What's Wrong?) and discuss what the skit taught them about a specific social skill.

The enclosed CD also contains posters for each of the 21 social skills (and their steps) you will be teaching through these skit activities. Print the posters and display them in your classroom so students have a quick reference to the skills and their steps.

TITLE

BASIC INTERACTIONS

AUTHOR   DODD

SECTION	SCENE	TAKE
1		

SKILL 1

Following Instructions

TAKE 1

NARRATOR: TAKE ONE – *The class is filing into Mrs. Jones' room. Everyone is talking and laughing. All the students sit down except Mary.*

MRS. JONES: Mary, I'd like you to go back to your seat now so we can get class started.

MARY: *(Ignores the teacher and keeps talking to her friend.)*

MRS. JONES: *(A little more sternly.)* Mary, I asked you to sit down.

MARY: *(Rolls her eyes and moves slowly toward her seat; replies in a snotty tone.)* I'm going.

MARY: *(Sits down but continues to "mouth" words toward her friend.)*

NARRATOR: *And freeze. What's wrong here?*

 Have students discuss what they have seen, naming the inappropriate behaviors and decisions.

SKILL 1

Following Instructions

TAKE 2

NARRATOR: TAKE TWO – *Mary is standing by Jane's seat as the students file into class. Everyone sits down except Mary.*

MRS. JONES: Mary, I'd like you to go back to your seat now so we can get started with class.

MARY: *(Looks at the teacher.)* Okay, Mrs. Jones.

(Mary moves to her seat, sits down and gets her book out.)

MRS. JONES: Okay class, let's get going. Get your social studies book out and turn to page 450 please. Then everyone look up here.

MARY: *(Opens her book and looks up at Mrs. Jones.)*

MRS. JONES: Great job, everyone. Mary, would you begin reading?

NARRATOR: *And freeze. So, what's right here?*

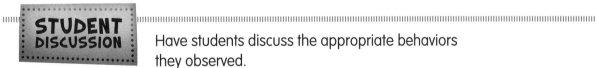

STUDENT DISCUSSION   Have students discuss the appropriate behaviors they observed.

What's right and wrong about the scenes on the previous pages? Answer below.

What's Wrong?

_____

_____

_____

_____

_____

_____

_____

_____

_____

_____

What's Right?

_____

_____

_____

_____

_____

_____

_____

_____

_____

_____

Following Instructions

Have students partner up. One partner from each team stays in the room with a predetermined object and one leaves. The first partner hides his/her object in the room, then writes detailed instructions for how to find it. When the other partner returns to the room, he/she reads the instructions and attempts to locate the item. After it is found, the partners switch and repeat the activity.

Write out a set of instructions. Then read the instructions out loud to the students and ask them to try to remember the instructions. Give students a set time to rewrite the instructions in order and determine what they are instructions for (baking a cake, getting to the mall from school, walking to the library from the classroom, getting to lunch).

SKILL 2

Greeting Others

TAKE 1

NARRATOR: TAKE ONE – *Mrs. Smith, the teacher, is standing by the front door of the school as students arrive.*

MRS. SMITH: Good morning, Katie!

KATIE: *(Looks the other way and walks on.)*

NARRATOR: TAKE ONE AGAIN.

MRS. SMITH: Good morning, Katie!

KATIE: *(Mumbles, doesn't look at Mrs. Smith and walks on.)* Morning.

NARRATOR: TAKE ONE, ONE MORE TIME.

MRS. SMITH: Good morning, Katie!

KATIE: *(Doesn't look at Mrs. Smith.)* S'up?

NARRATOR: *And freeze, freeze and freeze. What's wrong with Katie's behaviors in all of these situations?*

10

SKILL 2

Greeting Others

TAKE 2

NARRATOR: TAKE TWO – *Mrs. Smith, the teacher, is standing by the front door of the school as students arrive.*

MRS. SMITH: Good morning, Katie!

KATIE: *(Looks at Mrs. Smith.)* Hi, Mrs. Smith. How are you?

MRS. SMITH: I'm fine, thanks. Have a good day.

NARRATOR: *And freeze. So, what's right about this scene?*

STUDENT DISCUSSION

Include in this discussion the importance of greeting people by name if you know their names. This seems to be a skill that is greatly lacking in students. Another way to easily practice this skill is for the teacher to stand at the door as students enter and greet each student by name. Students should be prepared to greet the teacher by name.

What's right and wrong about the scenes on the previous pages? Answer below.

What's Wrong?

_____

_____

_____

_____

_____

_____

_____

_____

_____

What's Right?

_____

_____

_____

_____

_____

_____

_____

_____

_____

CLASS DISCUSSION

Make a picture sheet of the teachers your students see every day at school. Have the students write the names of those individuals next to their pictures. Then have them practice greeting the teachers using their correct names and titles. You may be surprised at how many names they really don't know.

Greeting Others

ACTIVITY 1

Challenge your students to greet adults they see this week and keep track of what the adults said and how they responded. Have students share their experiences with the class. This could also be done by having students greet five people they don't know in the school and keeping records to share with the class.

ACTIVITY 2

Ask each student to write a paragraph explaining why it is important to learn to greet others politely. Have students discuss why this is important to their future.

SKILL 3

Getting the Teacher's Attention

NARRATOR:	TAKE ONE – *The students in class are quietly working as the teacher moves around the room, providing one-on-one help. Jordan needs help and wants Mr. Howard to come over to him.*
JORDAN:	*(Raises his hand but Mr. Howard doesn't see him.)*
JORDAN:	*(Clears his throat and continues to raise his hand, but Mr. Howard is helping someone else.)*
JORDAN:	*(Begins making "grunting noises" and waving his hand around, but Mr. Howard is still helping someone else. Now Jordan is beginning to get angry.)*
JORDAN:	*(Blurts out.)* Mr. Howard, I need help.
MR. HOWARD:	One minute please.
JORDAN:	*(Sighs loudly, then lays his head down on his desk and continues to wave his hand.)*
MR. HOWARD:	*(Turns to Jordan.)* Okay Jordan, your turn.
JORDAN:	*(In a snotty voice.)* Finally!
NARRATOR:	*And freeze. Wow! What's wrong here?*

STUDENT DISCUSSION   Have students discuss Jordan's behaviors and attitude.

14

SKILL 3

Getting the Teacher's Attention

TAKE 2

NARRATOR: **TAKE TWO** – *The students in class are quietly working as the teacher moves around the room, providing one-on-one help. Jordan needs help and wants Mr. Howard to come over to him.*

JORDAN: *(Raises his hand, then notices that Mr. Howard isn't looking at him and is helping someone else. He lowers his hand and waits until Mr. Howard turns around.)*

JORDAN: *(Raises his hand again and looks at Mr. Howard.)*

MR. HOWARD: Jordan, do you have a question?

JORDAN: Yes, I need some help.

MR. HOWARD: Okay, just a minute. Let me finish over here.

JORDAN: Okay, thanks.

NARRATOR: *And freeze. So, what's right about the way Jordan handled this situation?*

What's right and wrong about the scenes on the previous pages? Answer below.

What's Wrong?

_____

_____

_____

_____

_____

_____

What's Right?

_____

_____

_____

_____

_____

_____

WHAT TO DO

Have the students discuss and practice voice tone. Some students may answer or speak in a "snotty" tone and not really realize it. Have students read the following statements in these voice tones: kind, snotty, whiny, angry and sad. Have students listen for the differences and discuss how people will react to each tone.

1. Can you help me?
2. I need help.
3. Mary is bothering me.
4. What are you doing?
5. Be quiet.
6. Pass me that pencil.
7. Why did I get a "C" on this paper?

Have your students role-play getting your attention.

Getting the Teacher's Attention

Have students make a "tip sheet" for younger students on how they should appropriately get a teacher's attention. Then have them do a presentation and teach this skill to a younger class.

Have students write and perform a skit showing the wrong way to get the teacher's attention. As the skit is acted out, have the students in the audience jot down incorrect behaviors. Discuss and have students make suggestions about how they would change the skit to make it more positive. Then choose students from the audience to act out the revised version of the skit.

NARRATOR: TAKE ONE – *José and Zach are at Game Stop looking for a new game. José just knows he has seen the* Space Warriors *game in this store but he can't seem to find it. The clerk is busy with someone else, but Zach and José have to get going to make it to basketball practice on time.*

JOSÉ: I know I saw that *Space Warriors* game in here. Now, where is it?

ZACH: Maybe they're sold out.

JOSÉ: No, I saw a bunch of them a few days ago.

ZACH: Well, we've got to hurry because practice is gonna start in fifteen minutes.

JOSÉ: Let's just ask.

NARRATOR: *The clerk is talking to someone else about a game.*

JOSÉ: *(To clerk.)* Hey, can you tell me if you have *Space Warriors*?

CLERK: I'll help you in a minute.

JOSÉ: But I'm in a hurry. Do you have *Space Warriors*? Yes or no?

CLERK: I'll have to look when I'm done here.

JOSÉ: *(Looks at his watch, then at Zach.)* C'mon Zach. We don't want to buy it from this dumb store anyway.

NARRATOR: *And the boys stomp out. And freeze. Would you consider this to be rude? Do you think the clerk should have responded differently? What about the boys?*

Getting Another Person's Attention

TAKE 2

NARRATOR: TAKE TWO – *José and Zach are at Game Stop looking for a new game. José just knows he has seen the* Space Warriors *game in this store but he can't seem to find it. The clerk is busy with someone else, but Zach and José have to get going to make it to basketball practice on time.*

JOSÉ: I know I saw that *Space Warriors* game in here. Now, where is it?

ZACH: Maybe they're sold out.

JOSÉ: No, I saw a bunch of them a few days ago.

ZACH: Well, we've got to hurry because practice is gonna start in fifteen minutes.

JOSÉ: Let's just ask.

NARRATOR: *The clerk is talking to someone else about a game.*

JOSÉ: Oh, he's busy. We'll just wait here until he's done.

NARRATOR: *The boys stand so the clerk can see they need help but they don't say anything.*

ZACH: *(Looks at his watch.)* We're gonna have to go.

JOSÉ: Okay. *(Looks at the clerk.)* Excuse me. I don't want to interrupt, but can you just tell me if you have *Space Warriors*? We have to get back to school.

CLERK: Sorry, we sold out of those yesterday. There should be more in a couple of days.

JOSÉ: Okay, thank you and sorry for bothering you. *(To Zach.)* Darn, we'll have to check back next week.

NARRATOR: *And freeze. What did you see in this scene that was polite and considerate?*

What's right and wrong about the scenes on the previous pages? Answer below.

What's Wrong?   # What's Right?

_____   _____

_____   _____

_____   _____

_____   _____

_____   _____

_____   _____

_____   _____

_____   _____

WHAT TO DO

Have students practice with a partner to get the attention of the following people:

- The teacher in class
- The principal in the hallway
- A fellow student who is standing in a group
- The lady who works at The Buckle

Getting Another Person's Attention

Have each student write a step-by-step description of how to appropriately get another person's attention. Write each step on a foot cut-out. Have students compare their steps.

Have students write and illustrate a comic book entitled *Ann and Andy Need Attention*. Have them show Ann trying to get a person's attention in the correct way and Andy trying to get a person's attention in inappropriate ways.

Introducing Yourself

TAKE 1

NARRATOR: TAKE ONE – *It's February and a new boy has come to middle school. Mark, Eduardo and other kids walk into class and see Thomas, the new boy, sitting at a desk.*

MARK: Who's that kid?

EDUARDO: I don't know his name but I know he's new. He came out of the guidance office this morning and took a tour with the counselor.

MARK: *(Loudly whispers to Eduardo.)* Looks kind of weird, doesn't he?

NARRATOR: *The new boy turns around and looks at them.*

MARK: Hey, what are you lookin' at, new kid?

NARRATOR: *And freeze. Have you ever been a new student? How did it feel? How do you think the new boy felt when Mark was so rude? Why would Mark act this way?*

NARRATOR: TAKE TWO – *It's February and a new boy has come to middle school. Mark, Eduardo and the other kids walk into class and see Thomas, the new boy, sitting at a desk.*

MARK: Who's that kid?

EDUARDO: I don't know his name but I know he's new. He came out of the guidance office this morning and took a tour with the counselor.

MARK: *(Walks up to the new boy, looks at him and smiles.)* Hi, my name is Mark and this is Eduardo. Are you new?

BOY: Yeah, my name is Thomas. I just moved here from California.

MARK: Wow, California. That must have been cool.

THOMAS: It was but my Dad got a new job, so here I am.

MARK: Well, I'm glad you're here. This is a pretty good school. Hey, would you like to eat lunch with us?

THOMAS: Sure.

MARK: Okay, just meet us by the cafeteria door and we'll show you how it works.

THOMAS: Thanks!

TEACHER: Okay class, take your seats now and we'll get started.

MARK: Nice to meet you. See you later.

NARRATOR: *And freeze. Name the things Mark did in this scene to be a person of character and make the new boy feel welcome and less nervous.*

What's right and wrong about the scenes on the previous pages? Answer below.

What's Wrong?

What's Right?

_____   _____

_____   _____

_____   _____

_____   _____

_____   _____

_____   _____

_____   _____

_____   _____

CLASS DISCUSSION

Point out to students that in this scene, Mark didn't shake Thomas' hand. In some situations, however, you would shake a person's hand when introducing yourself. Have students name some of those situations.

Have students practice shaking hands while saying, "Hi, my name is _____."

Introducing Yourself

Ask various adults and students who are not in your class to come into your room. Instruct your students to approach these people one at a time, shake hands and introduce themselves. Afterwards, debrief by talking about how your students felt introducing themselves to strangers or people they did not know very well.

Make arrangements with the secretaries, teacher aides, lunch people, administrators, custodians or other teachers in your building to have your students come to where they are working at a convenient time. Instruct your students to make eye contact, shake hands and introduce themselves. Give the adults a ranking form and have them grade your students' introductory skills on a 1-to-5 point scale (5 is the highest) and write down any constructive comments. Share the forms with your students and talk about how they did and how they felt while doing this task.

SKILL 6

Talking with Others

TAKE 1

NARRATOR: TAKE ONE – *José walks up the hallway to where Maria is standing.*

JOSÉ: Hi, Maria. How are you today?

MARIA: *(Looks down and mumbles.)* Okay, I guess.

JOSÉ: Did you get all the math homework done last night?

MARIA: *(Avoids looking at José.)* Yes.

JOSÉ: So are you going to the movies with us on Saturday night? It should be fun and….

MARIA: *(Interrupts José, looks down the hall and yells.)* Hey Brittany, wait a minute for me! *(Walks off without looking at Jose.)*

NARRATOR: *And freeze. What's your first impression of Maria's behavior? Does it seem rude to you? How would you change Maria's behavior to make it more acceptable?*

SKILL 6

Talking with Others

TAKE 2

NARRATOR: TAKE TWO – *José walks up the hallway to where Maria is standing.*

JOSÉ: Hi, Maria. How are you today?

MARIA: *(Looks at José.)* Hi, José. Oh, I'm fine. A little tired.

JOSÉ: Me too. Did you get all that math homework done last night?

MARIA: Yes, finally. It was pretty tough, didn't you think?

JOSÉ: I thought it was. I'm glad tomorrow is Friday. Are you going to the movies with us this weekend?

MARIA: Yes, I am. It should be lots of fun. I wonder if Brittany is going. *(Looks down the hallway.)* Hey, there she is. Let's go ask her.

NARRATOR: *And freeze. What's the big difference between Take One and Take Two?*

What's right and wrong about the scenes on the previous pages? Answer below.

What's Wrong?   # What's Right?

_____   _____

_____   _____

_____   _____

_____   _____

_____   _____

_____   _____

_____   _____

_____   _____

CLASS DISCUSSION

Have students write three questions they could ask these individuals to get a conversation going.

- Their math teacher

- A new student

- Their friend's mom, who is giving them a ride home

- Their grandma

Talking with Others

Ask the students in the class to get up, "mingle" and find out one interesting fact about each person in the class. Have the students write these facts down so they can share them with the class later. Discuss the phrase "making small talk," and share why it's sometimes hard, especially with people you don't know well.

Ask each student to give a two-minute talk about himself or herself. Ask listeners to be ready to ask the speaker a question to elaborate on what he or she has said. Discuss how asking people questions is an important part of conversation. Talk about listening, then about asking others to elaborate.

SKILL 7 — Making a Request

TAKE 1

NARRATOR: TAKE ONE – *Jamie has a cold and cough but does not have a tissue. He asks Mr. Williams, his teacher, for one.*

JAMIE: *(Walks up to Mr. Williams, coughing and sneezing.)* I need a Kleenex.

MR. WILLIAMS: There are tissues on that counter. Help yourself.

JAMIE: *(Walks over to the counter and grabs one. Walks off without looking at Mr. Williams or saying anything.)*

NARRATOR: *And freeze. What do you think about the way Jamie handled making that request?*

NARRATOR: TAKE TWO – *Jamie has a cold and a cough but does not have a tissue. He asks Mr. Williams, his teacher, for one.*

JAMIE: *(Walks up to Mr. Williams and coughs into his arm.)* Mr. Williams, may I have a Kleenex, please?

MR. WILLIAMS: Sure, there are tissues on the counter. Help yourself.

NARRATOR: *Jamie takes a Kleenex.*

JAMIE: Thank you.

MR. WILLIAMS: No problem.

NARRATOR: *Did you see some differences in the way this request was made? What was different?*

STUDENT DISCUSSION

NARRATOR: *Now, let's look at how Jamie makes a request in a different setting. This time, students are passing through the lunch line. Take One.*

JAMIE: (To the lunch lady.) Hey, can I have another scoop of macaroni and cheese?

LUNCH LADY: No, I'm sorry. You only get one scoop per lunch.

JAMIE: You gotta be kidding me! I'm paying too much for that little bit of food. That sucks!

LUNCH LADY: Well, I'm sorry you feel that way but there's nothing I can do about it.

JAMIE: Yeah, right. *(Gives the lady a dirty look and stomps off.)*

NARRATOR: *What did you think about that? Have you seen students react like that when a request has been turned down? Tell us about those times.*

STUDENT DISCUSSION

NARRATOR: **TAKE TWO** – *Students are passing through the lunch line.*

JAMIE: Can I have another scoop of macaroni and cheese?

LUNCH LADY: No, I'm sorry. You only get one scoop per lunch.

JAMIE: Darn, I really like that stuff. Oh well. Thanks. I may have enough money to get a second lunch.

LUNCH LADY: I'm glad you like it!

NARRATOR: *Did that look better? What positive changes did you see in this situation?*

What's right and wrong about the scenes on the previous pages? Answer below.

What's Wrong?

What's Right?

_____

_____

_____

_____

_____

_____

_____

_____

_____

_____

Making a Request

Thumbs up/Thumbs down. Ask students to respond to the following comments by asking themselves the question, "Would this or would this not be a part of making a proper, polite request?" Thumbs up if it would, thumbs down if it would not.

- Give me
- May I
- I'm going to
- Thank you
- Please
- Why not
- Right now
- I deserve
- I would like you to

Record (audio or video) examples of students making requests, then play them back and decide whether each student gets a plus or a minus. Each student audience member should have a card with a plus sign on one side and a minus sign on the other to hold up. Discuss why students judge the way they do.

TITLE INTERMEDIATE INTERACTIONS

AUTHOR DODD

TAKE

SECTION SCENE

2

NARRATOR:	TAKE ONE – *In this skit, the history class has been given a big study guide to complete. It is now working time. Lauren wants to concentrate and get this done so she doesn't have to take it home tonight. The problem is that she's in a class with several friends and is tempted to talk instead. During some of this skit, Lauren is talking to herself in her own mind.*
MR. WILLIAMS:	Okay class, you have 40 minutes left before the bell, so get busy and work on the assignment. It's due tomorrow.
LAUREN:	*(To self.)* Okay, I need to get this thing done. I want to go to Steph's house tonight and not have to worry about homework. So, c'mon Lauren, first get out the book and find Chapter 12.
STACY:	Lauren, come sit by us. Mr. Williams doesn't care.
LAUREN:	*(To self.)* Not a good idea. Stay here and get to work! *(To Stacy.)* Okay, let me get my stuff.
NARRATOR:	*Lauren moves over by Stacy.*
STACY:	*(Whispering.)* So, are you going to the dance on Friday night?
LAUREN:	*(Trying to start to work.)* Yeah, I think so.
STACY:	I think Max wants to dance with you.

LAUREN: *(Distracted now.)* Really! Who told you that? Max? Oh my gosh… tell me more.

STACY: Well, Max told Steph, who then told Mary, who told me, so I thought I should tell you.

LAUREN: This is so exciting! What should I wear?

MR. WILLIAMS: Girls, are you working on your study guides?

....

NARRATOR: *And freeze. Was Lauren doing what she said she was going to do? What was her first mistake? What should she have done? Do you think she will complete the study guide now?*

....

Staying on Task

NARRATOR: TAKE TWO – *In this skit, the history class has been given a big study guide to complete. It is now working time. Lauren wants to concentrate and get this done so she doesn't have to take it home tonight. The problem is that she's in a class with several friends and is tempted to talk instead. During some of this skit, Lauren is talking to herself inside her own mind.*

MR. WILLIAMS: Okay class, you have 40 minutes left before the bell, so get busy and work on the assignment. It's due tomorrow.

LAUREN: *(To self.)* Okay, I need to get this thing done. I want to go to Steph's house tonight and not have to worry about homework. So, c'mon Lauren, first get out the book and find Chapter 12. *(She does that.)*

STACY: Lauren, come sit by us. Mr. Williams doesn't care.

LAUREN: *(To self.)* Not a good idea. Stay here and get to work! *(To Stacy.)* Thanks Stacy, but I really need to get this thing done. I'll move over in a while.

STACY: Okay, Brainiac!

LAUREN: *(To self.)* Okay, now these questions come from section one so I'll do them first. *(Starts working.)*

STACY: Pssst… Lauren. Are you going to the dance on Friday?

LAUREN: *(Pretends not to hear.)* Now, question 5… section two.

STACY: Lauren.

LAUREN: Talk to you later. *(To self.)* Okay, six down and fifty more to go!

NARRATOR: *And freeze. It was pretty hard for Lauren to keep working when her friend wanted to talk. Do you ever have this problem? What techniques do you have to keep yourself on task?*

What's right and wrong about the scenes on the previous pages? Answer below.

What's Wrong?

_____

_____

_____

_____

_____

_____

_____

_____

What's Right?

_____

_____

_____

_____

_____

_____

_____

_____

CLASS DISCUSSION

Have students write down some responses they could use when someone tries to distract them from their work.

Staying on Task

Ask students to prepare a front page of a tabloid magazine (you may need to discuss what this is) with suggestions for staying on task. Include words and pictures. Tell students it will need to have "STUDENTS STAY ON TASK!!!" as the heading.

Assign each student an accountability partner who will quietly remind them to return to their task if they stray off. You can use a code like "RTT" (return to task) so they don't have to come up with their own reminder. Give a prize at the end of the week to students who didn't have any reminders.

If you would rather not have students do this, you can divide the class into teams of two or three and let them know that you will be placing a sticky note on the desks of students who are off task. That would be a negative point for the team. (Teams that turn their behavior around may be able to have negative points subtracted; this is at the teacher's discretion.) Keep track of those points and reward the groups with the lowest number of points at the end of the week.

NARRATOR: TAKE ONE – *This skit involves completing homework. Now be honest, who likes to do homework? Very few people! But we know completing homework is part of being successful in school. And why do we want that success? Because we want a good job, a nice place to live, a cool car and a comfortable life when we become adults. So let's first take a look at the don'ts of homework completion.*

Irresponsible Izzy is our first character. This is the kid who can't seem to get it together. Let's listen in on Izzy's struggle.

IZZY: I know there was homework in math and science but I forgot to write it down and now I can't remember what it was. Let's see, was it page 233 or 322 in math? I think I was talking to Jordan when the teacher gave that assignment. Let me see… where's that math book? Oh great, I forgot to bring it home. Oh well, maybe I can get it done before school in the morning. So, on to science. Okay, I think this is the worksheet. *(Shuffles through a pile of papers.)* I don't know why Mrs. James gives so much homework. It's just ridiculous. Oh well, I just need to get this done.

NARRATOR: *RRRing! RRRing! RRRing!*

IZZY: Hello? Oh, David! Hi. How are you? What are you doing? You're going to the park? Well, sure, I'd like to go. Do you have homework to do? Oh, you got it all done right after school. Well, good for you. Anyhow, yep… I'll meet you at the park. I'll just get my homework done later. See you in a few!

NARRATOR: *Two hours later.*

IZZY: Wow! Hanging out at the park really wore me out. I didn't realize it was this late and I still have that science to do. Where'd I put that worksheet? Oh, here it is. It's so long and I'm so tired. Maybe I'll just wait until morning to do it. I'll get up early. I'm going to bed.

NARRATOR: *A text comes in and Izzy ends up texting a friend for nearly an hour before falling into bed.*

NARRATOR: *Morning comes and the alarm rings. Ring!*

IZZY: Man, I wish I could sleep a little more. Maybe just once on the snooze.

NARRATOR: *Ring!*

IZZY: Oh my gosh, it's so late. I have to get to school or I'm going to be tardy.

NARRATOR: *So, Izzy gets to school and goes to her class.*

TEACHER: Class, please hand in the homework for today.

IZZY: Oh no!

NARRATOR: *So Izzy's homework is not done once again. What were some of the reasons she didn't get it done? Izzy made bad decisions and now she has to face the consequences.*

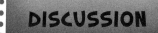

What's right and wrong about the scene on the previous pages? Answer below.

What's Wrong?

_____

_____

_____

_____

_____

_____

_____

_____

What's Right?

_____

_____

_____

_____

_____

_____

_____

_____

CLASS DISCUSSION

Ask the students what Izzy should have done. Ask what consequences they think she will have to face.

Ask students what their plan is for getting their homework done.

NARRATOR: TAKE TWO – *This skit involves completing homework. Now be honest, who likes homework? Very few people! But we know completing homework is part of being successful in school. And why do we want that success? Because we want a good job, a nice place to live, a cool car and a comfortable life when we become adults. So let's take a look at the do's of homework completion.*

Responsible Ryan is our next character. Ryan is a kid who wants to do his best and has set up a homework plan for himself that seems to work. Ryan wants to be a doctor someday and he knows that he has to start developing good study habits right now. Let's listen in on his situation.

RYAN: Wow! This is going to be a busy night. I have basketball practice after school and karate at seven. I better take a look at the old assignment book and see exactly what I have to take home. Okay, math assignment and I need the book. Check. Science worksheet. Got it and I need that book, too. No English tonight but I have a map to complete for history. I can do that without the book. Got it. So, I think that's all. I better get to practice before I end up sitting on the bench.

NARRATOR: *After practice, Ryan goes home. It's five o'clock.*

MOM: Do you have homework, honey?

RYAN: I have some so I better get on it. When's dinner?

MOM: About six o'clock. Want a granola bar to tide you over?

RYAN: Thanks, Mom.

NARRATOR:	*Ryan goes to his room and opens his backpack. He gets out his assignment book and the work he needs to do.*
RYAN:	Okay, I think I'll start with math, then go to science and do the map last cuz I need to use the computer.
NARRATOR:	*Ryan sits at his desk and puts the work to be completed in one pile. When he finishes an assignment, he checks it off in his assignment book and puts it back in his backpack in folders he has color coded for each subject.*
MOM:	Ryan, supper's ready. Come on down.
RYAN:	Coming, Mom. *(To himself.)* Okay, math done, science done and map completed. Done, done, done. I'm starving.
NARRATOR:	*So Ryan eats supper, goes to karate and comes home with no worries for tomorrow. He has a homework plan that includes making sure he has all of his homework before he leaves school, knowing what evening activities he has and getting the homework done before he goes to them. He also works carefully and neatly, and double checks to make sure he gets the completed homework back in his backpack. Ryan is preparing for his future, which looks very bright!*

What's right and wrong about the scene on the previous pages? Answer below.

What's Wrong?   # What's Right?

_____   _____

_____   _____

_____   _____

_____   _____

_____   _____

_____   _____

_____   _____

_____   _____

CLASS DISCUSSION

Have students make a poster they can put in their locker that spells out the steps of a good homework plan. Then remind them to look at it every day and follow it.

Completing Homework

Have students write a letter to a friend who is having trouble with his/her grades, giving advice for completing homework.

Have students make a cardboard "calling card" that has their name, grade and school name, and their plan for completing homework (see template on CD). Have them put copies of the card in their assignment book and locker.

NARRATOR:	TAKE ONE – *The teacher is in the middle of instructing the class in math.*

TEACHER: So, you can see, x-2=5 and then....

TORY: *(Raises his hand and waves it around.)*

TEACHER: Yes, Tory. Do you have a question?

TORY: Can I go to the office and make a phone call?

TEACHER: Well, not right now. We need to finish this lesson. You can go between classes.

TORY: *(Getting a little louder.)* But I need to call my mom.

TEACHER: I'm sorry, but like I said, not now. Now, let's get back to problem nine.

TORY: *(Hand in the air again.)* I need to call my mom now. *(Spoken loudly and rudely.)*

TEACHER: Tory, you cannot go now. Wait until homework time and I'll give you a pass.

TORY: I can't wait until then. I'm going to the office. *(Gets up and stomps out.)*

NARRATOR: And freeze. What's wrong here?

What's right and wrong about the scene on the previous page? Answer below.

What's Wrong?

_____

_____

_____

_____

_____

_____

_____

What's Right?

_____

_____

_____

_____

_____

_____

_____

CLASS DISCUSSION

Have students write a short paragraph explaining why arguing with the teacher is a bad idea.

Ask students how they could improve on the skill of Accepting "No" for an Answer?

NARRATOR:	TAKE TWO – *The teacher is in the middle of instructing the class in math.*

TEACHER:	So, as you can see, x-2=5 and then….
TORY:	*(Raises his hand.)*
TEACHER:	Yes, Tory. Do you have a question?
TORY:	*(Looks at the teacher.)* Mr. James, I'm sorry, but can I go to the office to use the phone?
TEACHER:	Well, not right now, Tory. We need to finish this lesson.
TORY:	Okay.

NARRATOR:	*Mr. James finishes the lesson.*

TEACHER:	Okay now guys, take the rest of the period to do your homework, questions 12 through 25. *(Returns to his desk.)*
TORY:	*(Walks up to Mr. James and talks in a quiet voice.)* Mr. James, can I use the phone now? I need to get a hold of my mom before she leaves for work.
TEACHER:	Sure, you can go now. *(Signs pass.)*
TORY:	Thank you.

NARRATOR:	*And freeze. So, what's right here?*

What's right and wrong about the scene on the previous page? Answer below.

What's Wrong?   # What's Right?

_____   _____

_____   _____

_____   _____

_____   _____

_____   _____

_____   _____

_____   _____

_____   _____

CLASS DISCUSSION

Have the students draw a cartoon with dialogue that illustrates the right and wrong ways to accept "No" for an answer.

Ask students if they think they have a problem accepting "No" for an answer. If so, is it worse at home, at school or somewhere else?

Accepting "No" for an Answer

Have students make a poster with the following words written vertically on the left side of the poster board, like this:

Accept

No

For

An

Answer

Have them use the first letter of each word to come up with a word that helps describe the correct way to use the skill. Students can use color and visuals if they want.

Have students write a letter to a younger child explaining why it's important to learn to accept "No" for an answer. Have them include reasons for the present and the future.

Disagreeing Appropriately

NARRATOR: TAKE ONE – *Courtney and Angelina are friends who want to spend Saturday afternoon together. Problems arise as they try to make plans.*

COURTNEY: So on Saturday, I'm thinking it would be fun to go to the mall and meet up with Jessica. I'm really anxious to stop in at Aeropostale and see what's on sale. Jessica said she could meet us there.

ANGELINA: *(Looks at Courtney.)* Oh, I guess I thought it was just you and me hanging out. Did Jessica ask to come?

COURTNEY: Well, yeah, she asked if she could come and I like her, so I thought it would be okay.

ANGELINA: I understand that. I know the two of you are friends, but to be honest with you, I feel kind of uncomfortable with Jessica. I feel like she doesn't like me, so I'm afraid it might not be too much fun for either of us. I was really excited about spending the day with you.

COURTNEY: Gosh, Ang, I didn't realize you felt that way about Jessica. Well, how about we go to the mall then I'll meet up with her later.

ANGELINA: That would be perfect, Courtney. Thanks!

NARRATOR: *And freeze. Let's share some thoughts about what happened this time. Do you think this plan will work? What do we mean by the word "compromise"? Are you a good compromiser?*

Disagreeing Appropriately

TAKE 2

NARRATOR: TAKE TWO – *Courtney and Angelina are friends who want to spend Saturday afternoon together. Problems arise as they try to make plans.*

COURTNEY: So on Saturday, I'm thinking it would be fun to go to the mall and meet up with Jessica. I'm really anxious to stop in at Aeropostale and see what's on sale. Jessica said she could meet us there.

ANGELINA: Oh, I thought it was just going to be you and me. Why does Jessica have to come?

COURTNEY: Well, she asked to come and I like her, so what's the big problem?

ANGELINA: Courtney, remember that she was talking behind my back last year? I feel uncomfortable around her.

COURTNEY: Well, what do you want me to do? I've already asked her. This is going to ruin our Saturday.

ANGELINA: No, it won't. Let's just go an hour early and you and I will hang out until it's time for you to meet up with Jessica. I'm fine with that. That way you can hang out with both of us and there won't be any drama.

COURTNEY: You're okay with that?

ANGELINA: Well, I think it's the best solution for now. Okay with you?

COURTNEY: Sure, I'll meet you at eleven.

NARRATOR: *And freeze. What do you think about this solution? Will it work? Is it realistic? Would you be willing to come to this compromise?*

What's right and wrong about the scenes on the previous pages? Answer below.

What's Wrong?

_____

_____

_____

_____

_____

_____

_____

What's Right?

_____

_____

_____

_____

_____

_____

_____

CLASS DISCUSSION

Have students discuss the following comments and decide whether they would be used to disagree appropriately or inappropriately.

- That's retarded

- I understand but....

- What are you thinking? (Could this be both?)

- I thought we were going to _____

- I feel uncomfortable

- That ticks me off

- That's stupid

- Why? (Think about this one!)

- Shut up

Disagreeing Appropriately

Divide students into groups and have them create a "20/20"-like news show on why kids disagree rudely with others. Have each group choose a master of ceremonies, a reporter and people who will be interviewed. Once the groups have developed their programs, have them present to the rest of the class.

Have students write and perform a rap song about disagreeing.

SKILL 12

Volunteering

TAKE 1

NARRATOR: TAKE ONE – *Mom and Jeff are at Grandma's house. Grandma has a number of boxes that need to be carried up to the attic but it's just too much for her. Grandma leaves the room.*

MOM: Jeff, these boxes are so heavy. It would be really nice if you would carry them upstairs for Grandma.

JEFF: I'm tired, Mom. I didn't want to come here today anyway. There are a million boxes and it'll take forever. I don't want to be here all afternoon. I want to go play video games with Mark and Craig.

MOM: Listen here, young man, you need to carry these boxes upstairs for your grandmother.

JEFF: *(Starts to argue.)* I don't want to....

NARRATOR: *He stops because Grandma comes back into the room.*

MOM: *(Gives Jeff the "evil eye.")*

JEFF: Uh, Grandma, I guess if you really need help, I could carry some of these boxes upstairs. *(He looks at his watch.)* I guess I have time.

GRANDMA: Oh, Jeff, that's sweet but you're busy. No, it's fine, I can get them later.

JEFF: Okay then.

NARRATOR: *And freeze. Do you think Grandma thought Jeff wanted to help her? Why do you think she said no? What was wrong with the way Jeff volunteered?*

59

NARRATOR: TAKE TWO – *Mom and Jeff are at Grandma's house. Grandma has a number of boxes that need to be carried up to the attic but it's just too much for her. Grandma leaves the room.*

JEFF: Wow! Grandma has a ton of heavy boxes in this room. What's she doing with all of this?

MOM: I think she wants to put them all in the attic.

JEFF: She can't carry these upstairs. They're way too heavy.

NARRATOR: *Grandma re-enters the room.*

JEFF: Grandma, these boxes are too heavy for you. I'd be glad to carry them up to the attic. I have some time and look at these muscles!

GRANDMA: *(Laughs.)* Wow, those are huge muscles all right! That's so nice of you, but don't you have plans for this afternoon?

JEFF: Oh, Mark and Craig and I are going to play video games but we can do that later. This won't take that long.

GRANDMA: Well, okay. I'd really appreciate the help.

JEFF: I'll do it now. You and Mom go take it easy!

NARRATOR: *Jeff finishes the job.*

JEFF: Okay, boxes all upstairs. Need anything else?

GRANDMA: Yes, I do.

JEFF: What?

GRANDMA: I need you to taste-test these chocolate chip cookies if you have time.

JEFF: Oh, I think I have plenty of time for that!

NARRATOR: *And freeze. What did you like about the way Jeff volunteered in this scene? Have you ever volunteered and made things easier for someone? Tell us about it.*

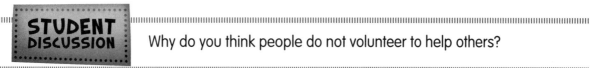

STUDENT DISCUSSION Why do you think people do not volunteer to help others?

What's right and wrong about the scenes on the previous pages? Answer below.

What's Wrong?   # What's Right?

_____   _____

_____   _____

_____   _____

_____   _____

_____   _____

_____   _____

_____   _____

_____   _____

CLASS DISCUSSION

Have students name some ways they could volunteer to help others.

- In their town:
- In their home:
- In their school:

Volunteering

Have students make a photo essay from magazine pictures depicting things people do to help others. Have them discuss how they can appropriately ask to help with various projects.

Have each student make a "postcard" with a message and picture that describes a time when they volunteered or helped others in some way.

SKILL 13

Making an Apology

TAKE 1

NARRATOR: TAKE ONE – *Talia and James are friends but Talia has just heard from another friend, Brad, that James is talking about her behind her back.*

BRAD: Hey, Talia, come here a minute. I need to tell you something.

TALIA: What's up?

BRAD: I hate to tell you this but I feel like I have to. Did you know that James is talking smack about you?

TALIA: What? About me? About what?

BRAD: He's telling people that you're trying to steal Karrie's boyfriend.

TALIA: Mark? Our families have been friends since we were in kindergarten. I was just talking to him yesterday about his older sister. She was in a car accident. I gave him a hug because he's upset about it.

BRAD: Well, James saw that conversation and thought something else was going on.

TALIA: I can't believe it! How could he do this to me? I thought we were friends.

BRAD: Well, you can ask him because here he comes now.

NARRATOR: *James walks up.*

JAMES: Hi guys. What's up?

BRAD: Not much. Well, I gotta go.

TALIA: *(Gives James a dirty look and says nothing.)*

JAMES: What's wrong with you?

TALIA: It's not what's wrong with me. It's what's wrong with you, James. Why are you telling people I'm trying to get Mark as a boyfriend?

JAMES: Well, I saw you two together yesterday so what am I supposed to think? You know Mark is going out with Karrie yet you're making the moves on him.

TALIA: Yes, I do know they're going out. But what you don't know is that Mark's family and mine have been friends forever. His sister was in an accident and I hugged him because he's upset about it. Then you stick your nose into it and start to spread rumors. Thanks a lot.

JAMES: Well, SORRY then Talia. Maybe that's true and maybe it's not, but one thing I know, you should keep your hands to yourself.

TALIA: And you should keep your big mouth shut. *(Turns and stomps off.)*

JAMES: *(Yells after her.)* I said sorry!

NARRATOR: *And freeze. Did it seem like James was really sorry for what he did? Why not? Do you think it's sometimes hard to make an apology? Talk about a time when you had to apologize.*

SKILL 13

Making an Apology

TAKE 2

NARRATOR: TAKE TWO – *Talia and James are friends but Talia just heard from another friend, Brad, that James is talking about her behind her back.*

BRAD: Hey, Talia. Come here a minute. I need to tell you something.

TALIA: What's up?

BRAD: I hate to tell you this but I feel I have to. Did you know that James is talking smack about you?

TALIA: What? About me? About what?

BRAD: He's telling people that you're trying to steal Karrie's boyfriend.

TALIA: Mark? Our families have been friends since we were in kindergarten. I was just talking to him yesterday about his older sister. She was in a car accident. I gave him a hug because he's upset about it.

BRAD: Well, James saw that conversation and thought something else was going on.

TALIA: I can't believe it! How could he do this to me? I thought we were friends.

BRAD: Well, you can ask him because here he comes now.

NARRATOR: *James walks up.*

JAMES: Hi guys, what's up?

BRAD: Not much. Well, I gotta go.

TALIA: *(Gives James a dirty look and says nothing.)*

JAMES: What's wrong with you?

TALIA: It's not what's wrong with me. It's what's wrong with you, James. Why are you telling people I'm trying to get Mark as a boyfriend?

JAMES: Well, I saw you two together yesterday so what am I supposed to think? You know Mark is going out with Karrie, yet you're making the moves on him.

TALIA: Yes, I do know they're going out. But what you don't know is that Mark's family and mine have been friends forever. His sister was in an accident and I hugged him because he's upset about it. Then you stick your nose in and start to spread rumors. Thanks a lot.

JAMES: *(Looks surprised.)* Oh my gosh, Talia! I didn't know that. I just saw the hug and I assumed. I guess I was all wrong. I'm so sorry. Please forgive me. I'll make sure I tell people I was wrong and get this cleared up.

TALIA: Well, I would appreciate that, James. I don't want Karrie all upset and people mad at me.

JAMES: Honestly, I'll take care of it. Just forgive me.

TALIA: Okay, I forgive you.

JAMES: Thank you so much for understanding. I'm an idiot!

TALIA: *(Laughs.)* No comment!

NARRATOR: *And freeze. Would you have forgiven James? Have you ever felt betrayed by a friend? Discuss a situation where you had to forgive. Is it possible to forgive and forget?*

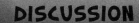

What's right and wrong about the scenes on the previous pages? Answer below.

What's Wrong?

_____

_____

_____

_____

_____

_____

_____

_____

_____

_____

What's Right?

_____

_____

_____

_____

_____

_____

_____

_____

_____

_____

Making an Apology

Have students write a poem about apologizing. It can be funny or serious. Have students read their poems aloud to the class. Then put all the poems in an "apology book."

Have students make up a situation in which they were wrong about something. Then have them write an apology note to the person they wronged. Have students read their notes aloud to the class and discuss the essential parts of apologizing.

SKILL 14

Being a Good Sport

NARRATOR:	TAKE ONE – *Being able to participate in activities is a fun part of school, but getting angry and being a bad sport can take the fun out of it. This scene takes place during middle school dodge ball season. Students are organizing their teams and playing their first games. Mike wants to play for the Dodgers.*
MIKE:	*(To the kids already on the Dodgers team.)* Hey you guys! I want to play on your team. You need a strong player and you know there's no one better than me. What do you say?
NARRATOR:	*The other kids look at each other. Obviously, they don't really want Mike on their team. He has a reputation of being a bragger and a poor sport.*
MIKE:	Come on. This is lame. You know you won't win without me. You guys are too small. You'll be sorry if you don't let me play with you.
STEVE:	We do need another person. So okay, Mike, you can be on our team. *(Other kids give each other sarcastic looks.)*
MIKE:	Great! So, we're up… Let's play!
NARRATOR:	*The first game begins.*
MIKE:	*(Yells at Steve.)* Hey, Steve, pass that ball to me. Quit hoggin' it!
NARRATOR:	*Steve throws the ball and misses the guy he's throwing it at.*

MIKE: Geez! What a lousy throw. Like a little girl. C'mon!

NARRATOR: *Another boy throws the ball and misses.*

MIKE: *(Blows up.)* What's wrong with you? Wimp!

NARRATOR: *A ball comes flying from the other side and hits Mike.*

OTHER TEAM: You're out!

MIKE: No, I'm not. It didn't hit me.

MR. HAMILTON *(teacher):* Yes it did, Mike. You're out.

NARRATOR: *Mike throws the ball down and stomps off in anger.*

STEVE: *(To other kids.)* I think we made a mistake having him on our team.

NARRATOR: *And freeze. Mike took all the fun out of playing dodge ball. What were some of the inappropriate things he did? Do you commonly see these kinds of things in school activities? Share some of the things you've observed.*

SKILL 14

Being a Good Sport

NARRATOR:	TAKE TWO – *Being able to participate in activities is a fun part of school, but getting angry and being a bad sport can take the fun out of it. This scene takes place during middle school dodge ball season. Students are organizing their teams and playing their first games. Mike wants to play for the Dodgers.*
MIKE:	*(To the kids already on the Dodger team.)* Do you guys need another player for your team? I don't have a team and I'd really like to play with you.
STEVE:	We need one more person so you are it!
MIKE:	Great! So, looks like we're up. Let's play!
NARRATOR:	*The first game begins.*
MIKE:	*(Yells at Steve as the ball comes hurtling toward him.)* Watch out, Steve!
NARRATOR:	*Steve ducks, grabs the ball and gets the other guy out.*
MIKE:	Great play!!!
NARRATOR:	*Another ball comes toward Mike and hits him. Mike puts the ball down and goes out. The game continues and the Dodgers lose.*

MIKE: Great game, you guys. That was close. We'll get them next time.

STEVE: Great game, guys!

NARRATOR: *And freeze. What differences did you see this time? Which Mike would you rather play with? Let's look at the rights and wrongs from both games.*

What's right and wrong about the scenes on the previous pages? Answer below.

What's Wrong?

_____

_____

_____

_____

_____

_____

_____

_____

What's Right?

_____

_____

_____

_____

_____

_____

_____

_____

CLASS DISCUSSION

Have students write down the names of the activities they participate in. Under each one, have them write whether they are a good sport or a poor sport and give some examples. Ask the students to really think about the things that make them mad and the behaviors they show. Are there things they need to change?

Being a Good Sport

Have students create a public service announcement or video for the morning announcements that features students talking about various social skills, including how to be a good sport.

Have students create a monologue for "Bobby the Bad Sport." Have each student read his or her monologue aloud, creating Bobby's voice. Then discuss what made Bobby such a bad sport in each one. Take the discussion one step further by having students talk about how Bobby could change.

TITLE COMPLEX INTERACTIONS

AUTHOR DODD

TAKE

SECTION SCENE

3

NARRATOR:	TAKE ONE – *This scene is set in Mrs. Jones' tenth-grade English class. Mrs. Jones is making an announcement.*
MRS. JONES:	Class, I have a big announcement this morning. The essay committee has read all the papers you wrote on being a person of character and the winner of the $50 prize has been chosen. This year's winner is Maribelle Gonzalez. Maribelle, come on up. *(Everyone applauds as she comes up and gets her award. Mrs. Jones shakes her hand.)*
	(The bell rings.) RING!!!!
MRS. JONES:	Class dismissed. See you all tomorrow.
NARRATOR:	*The students leave the room and Sonia approaches Maribelle, who is looking at her certificate.*
SONIA:	*(Loudly and sarcastically.)* Make way everyone for the queen of character! I should have known you'd win, Maribelle. Congratulations. You are always the teacher's favorite.
MARIBELLE:	*(Looks hurt.)* Thanks a lot, and you're just mean! Everyone knows I deserved it.
NARRATOR:	*And freeze. What emotions and behaviors do you see from both of these girls?*

SKILLS 15-16

Giving/Accepting Compliments

TAKE 2

NARRATOR: TAKE TWO – *This scene is set in Mrs. Jones' tenth-grade English class. Mrs. Jones is making an announcement.*

MRS. JONES: Class, I have a big announcement this morning. The essay committee has read all the papers you wrote on being a person of character and the winner of the $50 prize has been chosen. This year's winner is Maribelle Gonzalez. Maribelle, come on up. *(Everyone applauds as she comes up and gets her award. Mrs. Jones shakes her hand.)*

(The bell rings.) RING!!!

MRS. JONES: Class dismissed. See you all tomorrow.

NARRATOR: *The students leave the room and Sonia approaches Maribelle, who is being congratulated by others.*

SONIA: Congratulations, Maribelle. I'm so glad you won the prize. You really are a great writer plus a nice person, so you deserved it.

MARIBELLE: *(Smiles.)* Thanks so much, Sonia. I really appreciate it but I think you could have won. Your paper was terrific.

SONIA: Well, thanks. See you later!

NARRATOR: *And freeze. Name some of the things you heard Sonia doing when she congratulates Maribelle. What does Maribelle do when she accepts the compliment?*

What's right and wrong about the scenes on the previous pages? Answer below.

What's Wrong?

_____

_____

_____

_____

_____

_____

What's Right?

_____

_____

_____

_____

_____

_____

CLASS DISCUSSION

Have students write down what they would say to compliment the following:

- A boy who earned an A+ in math
- A girl with new glasses
- A student who held the door open for an older person
- Someone who just sang a solo at the school talent show

Have students write down what they would say if they received the following compliments:

- I really like your hair today.
- I'm so glad you got a part in the play.
- You are so good in English.

Giving/Accepting Compliments

The Swatter Game

Make a large game board that is covered with squares. Place the game board in front of the room. In each square, write a positive or negative comment that could be a response to a compliment or a compliment itself. Divide the class into two teams.

Have a player from each team come to the front of the room. Give each player a rolled-up newspaper, which is the "swatter" (a flyswatter works well, too). (You will want to remind students about your class rules for keeping hands, feet and objects to themselves.)

Have the two competing students stand with their backs to the game board. Then describe a "compliment" scenario. For example, you might say, "What would you say to someone who told you he liked your laugh?"

The students must remain with their backs to the board until you say, "Go!"

The students then should turn to the board and try to be the first one to "swat" (touch a square with the swatter) the most appropriate answer. The person who does so gets a point for his/her team. Then have two more students (one from each team) come forward and repeat the process. Continue until all team members have had a chance to play.

Possible Scenarios:

- A classmate gets the Student of the Week award.
- Your best friend gets the lead in a play.
- A girl comes to school with new glasses.
- Another student comes to school with a new haircut. You really don't like it.
- Your math teacher's wife had a new baby.
- Your teammate made the winning basket.
- You see your school principal in the parking lot of the grocery store. He has a new car.
- A fellow student gets a 100% on a really hard science test.
- You brought cookies for your math class.
- You see a kid do a big skateboard trick after school.
- You see another student hold the door open for a younger kid.

SKILL 17

Accepting Criticism or a Consequence

TAKE 1

NARRATOR: **TAKE ONE –** *The teacher is looking in his/her grade book as papers are being passed in.*

TEACHER: Mike, I'm missing page 221 from you. It was due yesterday, so since I don't have it, you'll need to come in after school tonight and get it done before you leave.

MIKE: I know I handed that in to you yesterday.

TEACHER: Well, I'm sorry, but I don't have it.

MIKE *(Getting louder.)* Then you must have lost it because I'm telling you, I turned it in yesterday!

TEACHER: Mike, please lower your voice. We'll discuss this after school.

MIKE: *(Loudly.)* I'm not staying after school. I have things to do and I'm not staying because you lost my paper. I did it once. *(Looks at the kid next to him and whispers loudly.)* Worthless!

NARRATOR: *And freeze. What's wrong here?*

82

SKILL 17

Accepting Criticism or a Consequence

TAKE 2

NARRATOR: TAKE TWO – *The teacher is looking in his/her grade book as papers are being passed in.*

TEACHER: Mike, I'm missing page 221 from you. It was due yesterday, so since I don't have it, you'll need to come in after school tonight and get it done before you leave.

MIKE: *(Looks at the teacher.)* Okay. Gosh, Mr. Thomas, I guess I forgot that one. I thought I turned it in. I'll stop in after school and finish it or maybe I'll find it in my folders. Sorry.

TEACHER: Thanks, Mike. It shouldn't take too long.

NARRATOR: *And freeze. What was right about this situation?*

What's right and wrong about the scenes on the previous pages? Answer below.

What's Wrong?   # What's Right?

_____   _____

_____   _____

_____   _____

_____   _____

_____   _____

_____   _____

_____   _____

_____   _____

_____   _____

_____   _____

_____   _____

Accepting Criticism or a Consequence

The Time Machine

Ask students to think of a time when they argued or disagreed with someone. Have them share the event and what was said. Then have the students "go back in time" and redo the situation in a cartoon strip, following the Boys Town skill of Accepting Criticism or a Consequence.

Role-play scenes

Have students act out the following scenes using the skill of Accepting Criticism or a Consequence:

1. A parent tells a child he/she is grounded for tonight.
    (Role-play both incorrect and correct responses.)

2. One friend criticizes another for being rude to a mutual friend.

3. A teacher tells a student he/she must come in for a lunch detention and can't eat lunch with friends.

4. A teacher gives constructive criticism to a student about a poem the student has written.

SKILL 18

Giving Criticism

TAKE 1

NARRATOR: TAKE ONE – *Tiffany and Tomás are working on an anthropology project. Tiffany is making a poster showing the mummification process, while Tomás is gathering information from the computer.*

TIFFANY: Okay, this poster is just about done. *(Holds up the poster so Tomás can see it.)* What do you think? Pretty good if I do say so myself!

NARRATOR: *The poster is sparse and missing information, but is artistically done.*

TOMÁS: *(Sarcastically.)* You think that's done? Really? That doesn't have enough facts for even a "C." Mrs. Collins is never gonna accept that, and I'm sorry, but I need a good grade. Come on Tiff, that looks terrible! You've got to do that over.

TIFFANY: You have got to be kidding me! I think this hits all the main points and at least I'm creative. Your part is boring with all your dull facts.

TOMÁS: I knew I should have done this project by myself.

TIFFANY: I wish you would have! *(Stomps off.)*

NARRATOR: *And freeze. Do you think it's hard to give criticism? How about taking it? Discuss what was wrong with the feedback Tomás gave Tiffany. What was wrong with her reaction?*

SKILL 18

Giving Criticism

TAKE 2

NARRATOR:	TAKE TWO – *Tiffany and Tomás are working on an anthropology project. Tiffany is making a poster showing the mummification process, while Tomás is gathering information from the computer.*
TIFFANY:	Okay, this poster is just about done. *(Holds up the poster so Tomás can see it.)* What do you think? Pretty good if I do say so myself!
NARRATOR:	*The poster is sparse and missing information, but is artistically done.*
TOMÁS:	Wow, the artwork on that looks great. I really like the colors you've used. You're a good artist, Tiff. The only thing I would say is, knowing Mrs. Collins, she's gonna want a ton of detail. Do you think you could put in some more facts in this section right here? *(Points it out on the poster.)* I think she would be impressed by more detail in the way they mummified people. I think I saw some things about that in this book that might help. *(Hands her a book.)*
TIFFANY:	You really think so? Well, Mrs. Collins does like detail. Let me look at that book. I think I can do that.
TOMÁS:	I'll work some more on my part, too.
NARRATOR:	*And freeze. Talk about the differences in the way the kids handled the Take One situation and this one.*

What's right and wrong about the scenes on the previous pages? Answer below.

What's Wrong?

What's Right?

_____   _____

_____   _____

_____   _____

_____   _____

_____   _____

_____   _____

_____   _____

_____   _____

CLASS DISCUSSION

Have students make a list of criticisms they have given or received and explain
how they handled them. If they could do it over, would they change the things
they said or the ways they reacted?

Giving Criticism

Have each student make a pamphlet entitled "How to Give and How Not to Give Criticism" that can be handed out at the guidance office. Have the class vote on the best one to be copied for the guidance counselors.

Have students pretend to be "Aunt Sally," the advice columnist. Have them write an answer to this letter to Aunt Sally.

Dear Aunt Sally,

Sometimes things come up and I feel like I have to speak up and criticize things my friends or classmates do or say. Often, they get mad at me. How can I give constructive criticism without being rude?

Signed, Wondering

Have students read their answers. If time permits, have each student write a letter to Aunt Sally asking for social skills advice. Have students exchange their letters and write an answer to the one they receive.

NARRATOR:	TAKE ONE – *Miguel and Jackson are going to the YMCA dance. They get to the Y a little early and are standing outside in the parking lot.*

JACKSON:	So, Miguel, I have a little surprise for you.
MIGUEL:	A surprise! What'd you do, buy me a car? That way we can drive to dances instead of walking.
JACKSON:	Nope, not a car but something fun anyhow. *(Jackson pulls something from his pocket. It's marijuana.)* So, how about we try this before the dance starts? Might make it a whole lot more exciting.
MIGUEL:	Is that weed? Where'd you get that?
JACKSON:	Never mind where I got it. I have it and we need to try it now, while there's no one out here.
MIGUEL:	Jackson, are you sure? If we get caught, we'll be in so much trouble.
JACKSON:	We're not getting caught. What's the matter? Are you chicken? Should I tell that Michelle girl you like that you're a big chicken? I could tell the whole class you're a little girl. That'd help your reputation with Michelle!
MIGUEL:	Stop it! No, I'm not chicken. But, come on. We've got to move over to the side of the building.
JACKSON:	Now you're thinking. Let's get this party started!

NARRATOR:	*And freeze. Why do you think Miguel decided to smoke with Jackson? Is this a realistic example of peer pressure? Why or why not? Give a realistic example.*

SKILL 19 — Resisting Peer Pressure

TAKE 2

NARRATOR: TAKE TWO – *Rachel and Tara are at the mall. Tara doesn't have much money but sees a necklace she really wants.*

TARA: Rachel, look at this cute necklace. Don't you love it?

RACHEL: I do! How much is it?

TARA: $12.50

RACHEL: Are you going to get it? You should, Tara. It looks so cute on you!

TARA: I can't. I only have six dollars.

RACHEL: Darn. *(Thinks a second, then whispers.)* Hey, I bet you could just slip that in your pocket. It's little. They'd never see it.

TARA: I can't do that. Really, Rachel, that's just wrong.

RACHEL: Come on, Tara. All the clerks are busy. They'll never know.

TARA: I'll know. *(Firmly)* Come on. Let's go spend my six dollars on ice cream.

RACHEL: I like that idea!

NARRATOR: *And freeze. Do you think it's hard to stand up against peer pressure? What techniques did you see Tara use?*

What's right and wrong about the scenes on the previous pages? Answer below.

What's Wrong?   # What's Right?

_____   _____

_____   _____

_____   _____

_____   _____

_____   _____

_____   _____

_____   _____

_____   _____

CLASS DISCUSSION

Ask students to name some good reasons they could use if they need to resist peer pressure. Ask how they would respond to the following situations:

- A friend wants you to lie to your parents and go to a party instead of the movies.
- Your friend asks to copy your homework.
- Your friend asks you to write something on Facebook that is not true because she is mad at another girl.

Responding to Teasing

NARRATOR: TAKE ONE – *Justin and Brad are standing in front of the school before the bell rings. John, another friend, walks up behind Brad and gives him a shove.*

JOHN: Hey, Stupid! What's up?

BRAD: Shut up, you jerk. Why do you do that every day? I'm sick of you being such a moron. Not only are you ugly, but you have no brain. Just stop it.

JOHN: Oh, pretty upset for someone who's so stupid!

BRAD: I said stop it, idiot.

JOHN: Okay, Stupid. Is that what you really want, Stupid? Whatever you say, Stupid!

BRAD: *(Shoves John down.)* Stop it you piece of crap!

NARRATOR: *And DEFINITELY freeze. What do you see going on here with both boys? Is one in the wrong and one in the right? Can you see anything right about this scene? What part does language play in this situation?*

SKILL 20 Responding to Teasing

TAKE 2

NARRATOR: TAKE TWO – *Justin and Brad are standing in front of the school before the bell rings. John, another friend, walks up behind Brad and gives him a shove.*

JOHN: Hey, Stupid. What's up?

BRAD: John, I want you to stop calling me that. It's not funny and I'm tired of it.

JOHN: Okay, Stupid. Whatever you say!

BRAD: Justin, I'm going in and get some breakfast. Want to go with me?

NARRATOR: *And the two boys walk off, leaving John standing there.*

SKILL 20 — Responding to Teasing

TAKE 3

NARRATOR: TAKE THREE (same scenario)

JOHN: Hey, Stupid. What's up?

BRAD: John, I want you to stop calling me that. It's not funny and I'm tired of it.

JOHN: Gosh, Brad, I was just joking. I'm sorry.

BRAD: Thanks, John. That name just makes me mad. Hey, how about all of us go in and have some breakfast?

JOHN AND JUSTIN: Sounds good./Okay.

NARRATOR: *And the three boys walk off together.*

SKILL 20 — Responding to Teasing

TAKE 4

NARRATOR: TAKE FOUR (same scenario)

JOHN: Hey, Stupid. What's up?

BRAD: John, I want you to stop calling me that. It's not funny and I'm tired of it.

JOHN: Okay, Stupid. Whatever you say.

BRAD: That name makes me mad so I'm asking you once and for all to stop it.

JOHN: OOOH, Stupid, it makes you mad. OOOH, I better watch out.

JUSTIN: Come on, Brad, stop it. That's enough. It's not even funny anymore.

JOHN: Who are you, Stupid Junior?

NARRATOR: *Brad walks off and goes to the counselor's office.*

BRAD: Mrs. Petersen, I have a problem. Can I talk to you about it?

NARRATOR: *And freeze. Now, go back to each scenario and talk about how the students handled each one. What do you think about Brad's responses in each scenario? Is there one response that was better than the others? Can you think of another way to respond?*

What's right and wrong about the scenes on the previous pages? Answer below.

What's Wrong?

_____

_____

_____

_____

_____

_____

_____

_____

What's Right?

_____

_____

_____

_____

_____

_____

_____

_____

CLASS DISCUSSION

Have students write a Take Five with different responses from the boys.

Responding to Teasing

Have students choose a partner and act out two interactions in which a person is being teased. One should be healthy, appropriate teasing between friends and one should be inappropriate teasing. Have the class decide which is which and discuss why.

Have students draw a sketch of what the perfect school would look like. Have them include a list of the rules and consequences the school would have about bullying and teasing if they were the principal. When everyone is finished, display the sketches and talk about the rules the students established and why.

SKILL 21 — Reporting Other Youths' Behavior

TAKE 1

NARRATOR:	TAKE ONE – *A bulletin is being read over the intercom by the principal, Mr. Wilson.*
MR. WILSON:	And one final announcement for today. We're having a problem with graffiti in the seventh-grade girls' restroom. Students, it's everyone's responsibility to keep our school looking nice, so if you have any information about this situation, please let an adult know. Thanks and have a good day!
NARRATOR:	*In the PE locker room, Becky and Yolanda start laughing.*
BECKY:	Did you see those drawings in the bathroom?
YOLANDA:	*(Loudly.)* Yeah, and everyone knows who did it.
NARRATOR:	*Kate and Joy overhear this and turn toward Yolanda.*
KATE:	Who?
JOY:	Yeah, who did it?
YOLANDA:	That Lily girl on team 7B. I saw her draw on the outside of a stall with a Sharpie.
GIRLS:	Oh my gosh!/You did?/I knew it!/She's such a weirdo!
YOLANDA:	*(Laughing.)* Yeah, she's a weirdo for sure.
NARRATOR:	*Mrs. Smith enters.*

MRS. SMITH: Yolanda, did I overhear you talking about the girls' restroom? Do you know who did it?

YOLANDA: Uh, no, Mrs. Smith, I don't know. We were just talking about something that happened at the mall. Right, girls?

GIRLS: Yeah, right.

MRS. SMITH: Okay then. I guess I was mistaken. But if you hear anything, let me know.

YOLANDA: Oh, I will.

(Mrs. Smith walks out.)

BECKY: Why didn't you tell her?

YOLANDA: I'm not a snitch! Sooner or later that weirdo will get caught, but I'm not telling.

NARRATOR: *And freeze. Let's discuss what Yolanda did. What do you think was right or wrong? Why? What does it mean to be a snitch? Why would a student not want to be considered a snitch? What's the difference between a snitch and a reporter?*

Reporting Other Youths' Behavior

TAKE 2

NARRATOR: TAKE TWO – *A bulletin is being read over the intercom by the principal, Mr. Wilson.*

MR. WILSON: And one final announcement for today. We're having a problem with graffiti in the seventh-grade girls' restroom. Students, it's everyone's responsibility to keep our school looking nice, so if you have any information about this situation, please let an adult know. Thanks and have a good day!

NARRATOR: *In the girls' locker room, Yolanda is getting ready for PE class.*

YOLANDA: *(Thinking to herself.)* Oh my gosh! I think I know who did that. I saw Lily in the restroom with a Sharpie.

NARRATOR: *Mrs. Smith enters the locker room.*

MRS. SMITH: Okay girls, let's hurry up and get dressed.

NARRATOR: *Yolanda walks up to Mrs. Smith.*

YOLANDA: *(Speaking quietly.)* Mrs. Smith, may I speak to you when everyone's gone?

MRS. SMITH: Sure, Yolanda. Just stop by my office.

YOLANDA: Okay, thanks.

NARRATOR: Later, in Mrs. Smith's office.

MRS. SMITH: What can I do for you, Yolanda?

YOLANDA: Well, you know the graffiti in the girls' restroom? I was in that restroom yesterday and I saw Lily from team 7B walking out with a black Sharpie. I saw the graffiti and it was in that kind of marker.

MRS. SMITH: Did she say anything?

YOLANDA: No, she was just laughing with another girl.

MRS. SMITH: Did you recognize that girl?

YOLANDA: Yes, it was Sammi Jones.

MRS. SMITH: Thanks so much for the information, Yolanda. I'll pass it on to Mr. Wilson. You did the right thing to report.

YOLANDA: Okay, thanks.

NARRATOR: *And freeze. In this scene, Yolanda reported what she saw. Do you think it was easy for her to do this? Why do you think she chose to report? Would you say Yolanda is a person of good character? Why or why not?*

What's right and wrong about the scenes on the previous pages? Answer below.

What's Wrong?   # What's Right?

Ask students to name some situations they think must be reported. Have them practice what they would say to report them in the correct way. Discuss what could be considered snitching or tattling and how these situations could be handled in other ways.

Reporting Other Youths' Behavior

Have students write and act out several "reporting" scenarios, some that are appropriate reporting and some that are tattling. Have students decide which ones are tattling and discuss why.

Have students write and act out a skit showing bad behavior. After the skit, talk to the students about accurate reporting. Hand out a "police report" (see template on CD) and have the audience fill out the report, reporting what they saw and heard during the skit. After everyone is finished, have students share their reports and talk about how accurate or inaccurate they were.

You can create your own skits or ideas to teach social skills or school rules and policies to students! Have fun! Let your students be part of creating them. The following pages offer a couple of examples of the types of skits that can help you teach/reinforce school rules.

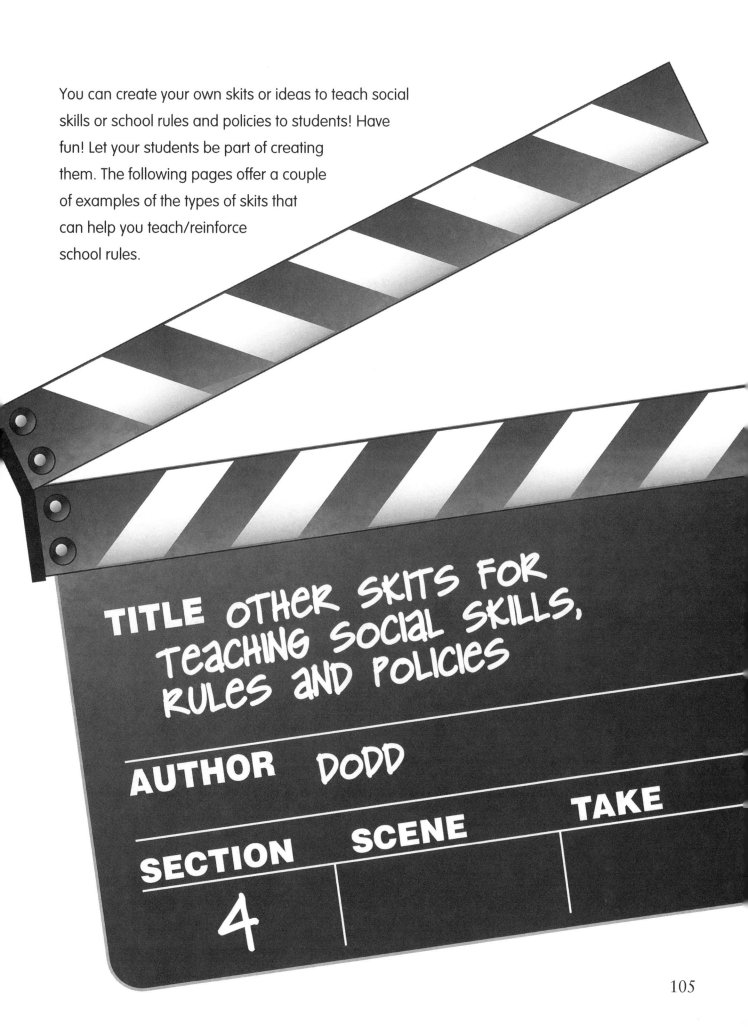

TITLE OTHER SKITS FOR TEACHING SOCIAL SKILLS, RULES AND POLICIES

AUTHOR DODD

SECTION 4

SCENE

TAKE

PDA Skit

TAKE 1

NARRATOR: *This scene opens at the football field. Jake and Ginger walk in.*

COACH: Why are you late?

CHEERLEADER: I know why. They were all mushy, gushy. *(Makes kissing gestures with hands.)*

COACH: *(In a stern voice.)* Get with the program, Jake.

JAKE: *(To Ginger.)* Wait for me on the sidelines.

GINGER: Okay. *(Wink!)*

CHEERLEADER: Jake and Ginger sitting in a tree, k-i-s-s-i-n-g.

JAKE AND GINGER: *(Make goo-goo eyes.)*

COACH: *(Yelling.)* Get your head in the game! Do your drills!!!

(Jake starts running, then turns and blows Ginger a kiss. Ginger catches it.)

STUDENT: Coach, Coach! They need you on the other side. There's been an injury.

COACH: I've got to take care of this so keep working. I'll be right back. *(Coach jogs off.)*

JAKE AND GINGER: *(Do "slow run" toward each other.)*

CHEERLEADER: *(Takes a photo of the couple with her phone and holds the photo up in front of them. From offstage, you hear:)* Yuck, they are sick!!

NARRATOR: *The moral of this story is…*

Showing PDA is definitely against our behavior code. It doesn't represent our school well and it doesn't represent you or your family.

PDA makes other people feel uncomfortable and will get you in trouble every time.

So remember, it's great to have friends. But public displays of affection are not appropriate anywhere, especially in school.

The Dress Code Skit

TAKE 1

ANA: The dress code says that girls' shorts and skirts must be fingertip length and boys' pants have to fit at the waist with no sagging. Boy, I remember a time when I first came here that I got in trouble about that. Do you remember that, Devon?

DEVON: Of course!
(Flashback…)

DEVON: Hey Ana. How's it going?

ANA: Hey Devon, I like your shorts. But let's just hope Mrs. Dodd doesn't notice them.

DEVON: Yeah, I thought they might be too short, but I really wanted to wear them.

BRYCE: Waz up! *(Pants are sagging.)*

ANA AND DEVON: Hi Bryce!

....

NARRATOR: *Mrs. Dodd comes outside.*

....

ANA: Hurry, it's Mrs. Dodd.

BRYCE: She's gonna see me sagging.

(They rush over to the group.)

ANA AND DEVON: Hide us!

(Mrs. Dodd slowly makes her way over to the group.)

MRS. DODD: Could I please talk to you guys?

DEVON, ANA, BRYCE: Sure./Okay.

MRS. DODD: Girls, those shorts are way too short for school, and Bryce, you need to pull up your pants. I really don't want you to wear those clothes to school again.

ANA, DEVON, BRYCE: Okay./Sorry.

MRS. DODD: Do you have any clothes you could change into?

ANA, DEVON, BRYCE: No.

MRS. DODD: Well then, you can borrow some pants from the office. It's the best we can do today.

ANA, DEVON, BRYCE: *(Look at one another, reluctantly replying.)* Okay.

(Camera fades out, then fades in to the kids wearing pants that are ugly.)

BRYCE: I think I'll rethink my school clothes.

DEVON AND ANA: Me too!

- -

NARRATOR: *The moral of this story is that there's a difference between the clothes you wear in the summer or on weekends and the clothes that are appropriate for school. Before coming to school, be sure you look at yourself in the mirror and ask yourself, "Are these school clothes and do they fit the dress code?" It's better to do that ahead of time than to get to school and have to be embarrassed. School is your job right now, so you have to dress for it.*

- -

Appendix: Skills and Their Steps

SECTION 1: BASIC INTERACTIONS

SKILL 1: **Following Instructions**

1. Look at the person.

2. Say "Okay."

3. Do what you've been asked right away.

4. Check back.

SKILL 2: **Greeting Others**

1. Look at the person.

2. Use a pleasant voice.

3. Say "Hi" or "Hello."

SKILL 3: **Getting the Teacher's Attention**

1. Look at the teacher.

2. Raise your hand calmly.

3. Wait to be acknowledged by the teacher.

4. Ask questions or make requests in a calm voice.

SKILL 4: **Getting Another Person's Attention**

1. Wait until the other person is finished speaking or is available to you.

2. Look at the other person.

3. Get that person's attention by saying "Excuse me...."

4. Wait until he or she acknowledges you. Say what you want to say.

SKILL 5: **Introducing Yourself**

1. Look at the person. Smile.

2. Use a pleasant voice.

3. Offer a greeting. Say "Hi, my name is...."

4. Shake the person's hand.

5. When you leave, say "It was nice to meet you."

SKILL 6: **Talking with Others**

1. Look at the person.

2. Use a pleasant voice.

3. Ask questions.

4. Don't interrupt.

SKILL 7: **Making a Request**

1. Look at the person.

2. Use a clear, pleasant voice tone.

3. Make your request in the form of a question by saying "Would you..." or "Please...."

4. If your request is granted, remember to say "Thank you."

5. If your request is denied, remember to appropriately accept "No" for an answer.

SECTION 2: INTERMEDIATE INTERACTIONS

SKILL 8: **Staying on Task**

1. Look at your task or assignment.

2. Think about the steps needed to complete the task.

3. Focus all of your attention on your task.

4. Stop working on your task only with permission from the nearby adult who gave you the task.

5. Ignore distractions and interruptions by others.

SKILL 9: **Completing Homework**

1. Find out at school what the day's homework is for each subject.

2. Remember to bring home necessary books or materials in order to complete your assignments.

3. Get started on homework promptly, or at the designated time.

4. Complete all assignments accurately and neatly.

5. Carefully store completed homework until the next school day.

SKILL 10: **Accepting "No" for an Answer**

1. Look at the person.

2. Say "Okay."

3. Stay calm.

4. If you disagree, ask later.

SKILL 11:   **Disagreeing Appropriately**

1. Look at the person.

2. Use a pleasant voice.

3. Say "I understand how you feel."

4. Tell why you feel differently.

5. Give a reason.

6. Listen to the other person.

SKILL 12:   **Volunteering**

1. Look at the person.

2. Use a clear, enthusiastic voice tone.

3. Ask to volunteer for a specific activity or task.

4. Thank the person and check back when the task is completed.

SKILL 13:   **Making an Apology**

1. Look at the person.

2. Use a serious, sincere voice tone, but don't pout.

3. Begin by saying "I wanted to apologize for..." or "I'm sorry for...."

4. Do not make excuses or try to rationalize your behavior.

5. Sincerely say that you will try not to repeat the same behavior in the future.

6. Offer to compensate or pay restitution.

7. Thank the other person for listening.

SECTION 3: COMPLEX INTERACTIONS

SKILL 14:   **Being a Good Sport**

1. Play fair and according to the rules.

2. Avoid fighting or criticizing others.

3. Remember to accept winning appropriately without bragging.

4. Remember to accept losing appropriately without pouting or complaining.

5. Thank the other players for participating.

SKILL 15:   **Accepting Compliments**

1. Look at the person who is complimenting you.

2. Use a pleasant tone of voice.

3. Thank the person sincerely for the compliment.

4. Say "Thanks for noticing" or "I appreciate that."

5. Avoid looking away, mumbling or denying the compliment.

SKILL 16:   **Giving Compliments**

1. Look at the person you are complimenting.

2. Speak with a clear, enthusiastic voice.

3. Praise the person's accomplishment, activity or project specifically.

4. Use words such as, "That's great," "Wonderful" or "That was awesome!"

5. Give the other person time to respond to your compliment.

SKILL 17:   **Accepting Criticism or a Consequence**

1. Look at the person.

2. Say "Okay."

3. Don't argue.

4. If given instructions or suggestions on how to correct the situation, follow them.

SKILL 18:   **Giving Criticism**

1. Look at the person.

2. Remain calm and use a pleasant voice tone.

3. Begin with a positive statement or some praise, or by saying "I understand...."

4. Be specific about the behaviors you are criticizing.

5. Offer a rationale for why this is a problem.

6. Listen to the other person's explanation. Avoid any sarcasm, name-calling or "put-down" statements.

SKILL 19:   **Resisting Peer Pressure**

1. Look at the person.

2. Use a calm, assertive voice tone.

3. State clearly that you do not want to engage in the inappropriate activity.

4. Suggest an alternative activity. Give a reason.

5. If the person persists, continue to say "No."

6. If the peer will not accept your "No" answer, ask him or her to leave or remove yourself from the situation.

SKILL 20:   **Responding to Teasing**

1. Remain calm, but serious.

2. Assertively ask the person to stop teasing.

3. If the teasing doesn't stop, ignore the other person or remove yourself.

4. If the teasing stops, thank the other person for stopping and explain how teasing makes you feel.

5. Report continued teasing or hazing to an adult.

SKILL 21:   **Reporting Other Youths' Behavior**

1. Find the appropriate adult or authority figure.

2. Look at the person.

3. Use a clear, concerned voice tone.

4. Specifically state the inappropriate behavior you are reporting.

5. Give a reason for the report that shows concern for your peer.

6. Truthfully answer any questions you are asked.